FURY
ON THE
BLISS FARM
AT
GETTYSBURG

John M. Archer

Ten Roads Publishing

Copyright ©2012 John M. Archer

All rights reserved. No part of this book may be reproduced in any form or by any electronic or mechanical means, including information storage and retrieval systems without prior permission of the publisher.

Printed and Bound in the United States of America
ISBN: 978-0-9837213-9-0

Fury On The Bliss Farm is based on an article by the author originally published in *America's Civil War*, July, 1995

First full-length edition by:
Ten Roads Publishing, LLC
P.O. Box 3152
Gettysburg, PA 17325
www.tenroadspublishing.com

Cover Design by Author

Contents

Preface	9
Acknowledgements	11
Introduction	13
JULY 1, 1863	16
JULY 2 – Morning	17
JULY 2 – Afternoon	27
JULY 3 – Morning	49
JULY 3 – Afternoon	59
Aftermath	60
Appendix A - Skirmishing	62
Appendix B - Wright's Breakthrough	64
Appendix C – Order of Battle	69
Endnotes	72
Index	79

Images

Gettysburg – 1858 Adams County Map	12
Map 1: Directions to Stop 1 Parking	14
Meade's headquarters at the Leister Farm (LC)	18
Map 2: Tour Stops	20
Brian farmhouse shortly after the battle (LC)	21
Brigadier General Alexander Hays (LC)	23
14th Connecticut monument circa 1880 (Page)	25
Bliss Farm as it appeared in 1863 (See Image Notes)(GNMP)	28
Maj. Gen. R.H. Anderson(B&L) / Brig. Gen. Carnot Posey(LC)	29
Close-up of Emmitsburg Road & Ziegler Farm 1869 (WAF)	29
Map 3: Bliss Farm &Vicinity 1863	32
View southwest toward Bliss Farm	33
Bliss barn as described by Chaplain Stevens (east face)	35
The 14th Connecticut marker at the barn site (Page)	38
Map 4: Situation around Bliss Farm: 6:30 pm	39
Brig. Gen Ambrose Wright (LC)	41
Modern view looks east toward Cemetery Ridge	44
Modern view of Cemetery Ridge and "Brown's Gate"	46
Map 5: Situation at Bliss Farm: 10:00 am, July 3	52
Maj. Theodore Ellis / Capt. Samuel Moore (Page)	53
Bliss barn as described by Chaplain Stevens (north face)	54
Connecticut marker at Bliss house site, circa 1891 (Page)	55
Union Skirmish Line Advances at Resaca in 1864 (HW)	62
Modern view of the rocky shelf on Cemetery Ridge	65

Image Notes:

B&L: <u>Battles & Leaders of the Civil War</u>, Robert Johnson and Clarence Buel (New York: Century Co. 1884-9)

GNMP: Gettysburg National Military Park

HW: Harpers Weekly Magazine

LC: Library of Congress

NA: National Archives

Page: <u>History of the Fourteenth Regiment, Connecticut Volunteer Infantry</u>, Charles Page, (Meriden: Horton Print Company, 1906)

WAF: Panoramic image from Soldiers National Cemetery courtesy of William A. Frassanito, <u>Early Photography at Gettysburg</u>

Cover Images: The front cover is based on a black & white photograph in the archives at Gettysburg National Park and shows the Bliss property as it appeared in 1863. The original painting by an unknown artist was in the possession of the Harris family (Bliss descendants) but has since disappeared. The author's research indicates the painting may well be one of a series of Gettysburg images painted by George Leo Frankenstein in 1866.
The back cover shows the Bliss Farm site in 2012.

Maps: The original maps included with the text are based on the 1869 Warren Survey Map and the 1876 Bachelder Map Series. Despite the extraordinary efforts of early surveyors to depict the battlefield, these maps all contain inconsistencies and errors. These base maps were combined with contemporary aerial photographs and field research to create the 1863 versions presented here.

"Great events sometimes turn on comparatively small affairs..."
Colonel William C. Oates, 1905*

Preface

The odd grassy mound between the long, low ridges south of Gettysburg might arouse the curiosity of a visitor, but the site of the Bliss Farm lies hundreds of yards from battlefield tour routes. Certainly, more infamous sites such as "Pickett's Charge," or the vista from the high ground at Little Round Top vie for one's attention, and the struggle for the once prosperous homestead is easily overlooked.

Yet, on July 2 and 3, 1863, the incongruously named farm was a no-man's land that changed hands some ten times – possibly more than any other ground at Gettysburg. While relatively limited in scope, the encounters on the Bliss Farm rose from a skirmisher's quarrel to a pitched battle that may well have helped turn the tide of the enormous Confederate assault of July 2.

Using a tour format, photos, maps, and first-hand accounts are used to allow the reader, both on the field and at home, to understand the struggle for this seldom visited area. Some of the contemporary accounts used to describe the actions here are inconsistent; one need only read a few Civil War memoirs to realize that combatants rarely agreed in their interpretations of battle. In the course of the text, the author has attempted to suggest a setting that allows these disparate versions to exist side-by-side.

While we follow the ebb and flow of this struggle, and its possible impact on the outcome of the battle, it is also a clear reminder that wars do not take place in a vacuum; despite this action's obscurity, the struggle would never be forgotten by any of those who fought here, the families of those who did not return, or the Bliss family.

Colonel William Oates was commander of the 15th Alabama at Gettysburg. Oates felt that his regiment's attack on Little Round Top held the key to Southern victory at Gettysburg. Ironically, the quote may more accurately reflect what occurred two hours later and almost two miles away.

Acknowledgements

My research on the struggle for the Bliss Farm has relied on information and support from a wide range of sources. First and foremost, acknowledgement is due to the long continuum of individuals and organizations, stretching from 1863 to the present day, without whose accounts this struggle would be but an enigma: the veterans of Gettysburg, whose statements are our best connection to the conflict; the research of Colonel John Bachelder, certainly the most dedicated historian of the battle; the records of the Park's overseers, from the Gettysburg Battlefield Memorial Association to the National Park Service; and finally, the contemporary research of modern historians Elwood "Woody" Christ and Harry W. Pfanz. A special thanks to Woody for his extensive research on William Bliss' life before and after Gettysburg; his efforts have brought the Bliss family's loss – and perseverance – into perspective. My appreciation goes as well to the staff at the Gettysburg National Military Park Library and at the United States Army Heritage and Education Center in Carlisle, Pennsylvania for allowing access to their extensive collections.

There are always those who, knowingly and unknowingly, ultimately make projects such as this come to fruition. My thanks to Ten Roads Publishing for their efforts to see this specialized study come to print. My greatest debt is to my wife Darlene who has supported my projects and patiently endured my obsession with Gettysburg. Without her love and understanding, this book would not have been possible.

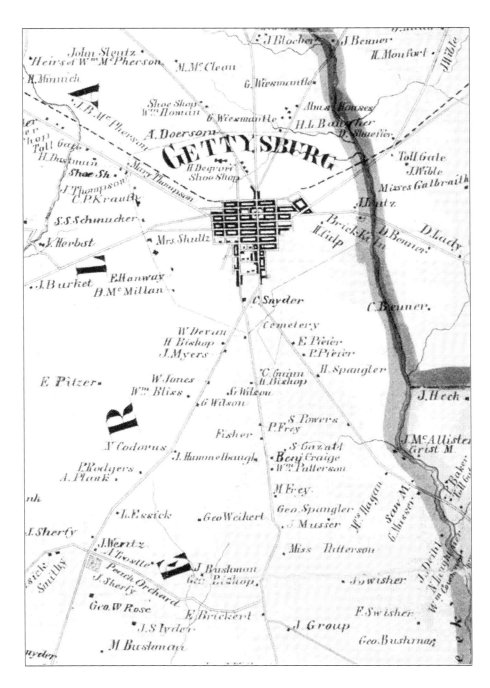

The busy crossroads of Gettysburg from the 1858 Adams County Map; William Bliss farm is at middle left

Introduction

In the *Gettysburg Sentinel* of August 11, 1856, the following real estate opportunity could be found:

A. Cobean offers farm at private sale with 44 acres a double log and frame house, weather-boarded, 2 wells of water near the house with pumps - a variety of fruit in the orchards include peaches and cherries.

The following April, one William Bliss would pay $1,960.96 for the small farm (later adding another seven acres for $182.50).

Born in southeastern Massachusetts in 1799, Bliss and his wife Adeline had settled for some twenty-five years in upstate New York near Jamestown. Over that time, however, the harsh winters of Chautauqua County no doubt contributed to the death of three of their six children. Perhaps drawn by the moderate climate of Southern Pennsylvania, William Bliss moved his wife and daughters Frances and Sarah to the thriving crossroads town named Gettysburg in 1857. There they no doubt expected to live out the rest of their days in peace; it was not to be. [1]

14

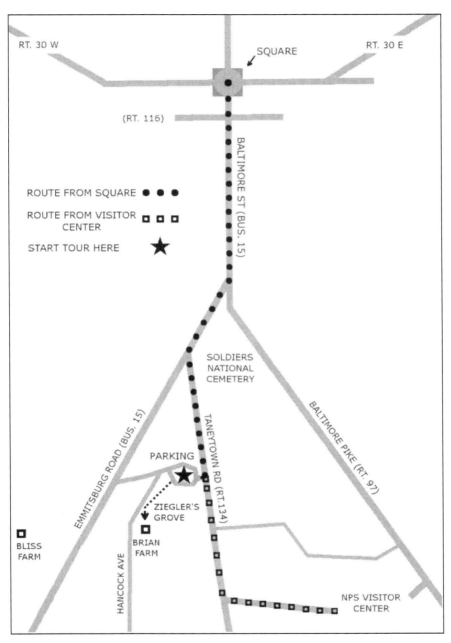

Map 1: Directions to Stop 1 Parking

STOP 1: CEMETERY RIDGE - ZIEGLER'S GROVE

This study of the struggle for the Bliss Farm begins with a brief description of the events leading up to the main action, accompanied by a walking tour of the area. The tour covers about one mile of relatively open ground, and some areas are uneven and can be wet. Proper footwear, sun protection, and insect repellant are strongly recommended.

For your convenience, Stop 1 can be reached from either the square in the center of Gettysburg (the roundabout at Rt. 30 & Bus. Rt. 15), OR from the National Park Visitor Center on the Baltimore Pike (See Map 1):

From the Square: Follow Baltimore Street (Bus. Rt. 15 South) for 1 mile and bear right onto Steinwehr Avenue. At the National Cemetery Annex (.5 mile), turn left onto Taneytown Road. Go <u>past</u> the main entrance to the National Cemetery at the crest of the hill (.5 mile), and then turn right into the next parking lot to park your vehicle.

From the Visitor Center: Drive west from the parking lots to the stop sign at the Taneytown Road exit. Turn RIGHT and follow the Taneytown Road about .25 mile, then turn LEFT into National Cemetery parking area to park your vehicle.

You may remain in your vehicle to read the following.

In 1863, the area east of the Taneytown Road where the National Cemetery now stands was an open height crossed by low stone walls; from the roadway, Gettysburg's Evergreen Cemetery and its formal brick gatehouse would be visible on the far side. The wooded area on the western side of today's parking lot was a more substantial stand of trees known as Ziegler's Grove.

JULY 1, 1863

The struggle that engulfed William Bliss' property during the battle at Gettysburg had its seeds in the bloody confrontation that began nearby on July 1, 1863. In the midst of a successful invasion of Pennsylvania that June, the Southern army under Robert E. Lee was forced to concentrate near the crossroads town of Gettysburg to confront the rapid pursuit by the Union Army of the Potomac. As that humid first of July wore on, advance elements of both armies clashed north and west of the town.

Yet, even while Federal troops double-quicked to battle through the fields past his home, Bliss, like many residents, chose to stay on his property as long as possible. However, by the time the fighting reached the Lutheran Seminary, less than a mile north of his property, Bliss had evacuated his wife and two daughters. When the family finally decided to leave, they left quickly, for "they left the doors open, the table set, the beds were made, apparently nothing had been taken out at all." The next occupants would be more tenacious.[2]

After eight hours of brutal conflict, the remainder of the Union First and Eleventh Corps – barely 9,000 men – retreated to two heights south of Gettysburg known as Cemetery Hill and Culp's Hill; there they anxiously awaited reinforcements. General Lee placed his army in a wide semi-circle around the Union position, anchoring his right flank on the ridge by the Lutheran Seminary west of town. His victory incomplete, Lee also awaited the arrival of fresh troops, confident he would drive the Union force from the high ground on July 2.[3]

That night, the low rumble of armies on the move broke the uneasy silence of the Pennsylvania countryside. For the time being, the fighting had rolled past the Bliss family's two-story house and enormous bank barn without the ruin visited on other farmsteads; but located in the broad valley southwest of Gettysburg, the farm now lay between the opposing armies.

JULY 2 – Morning

After the first day's conflict, Union commander Major General George G. Meade arrived near midnight, and spent most of the early morning hours studying the field, assigning positions for his rapidly converging corps. Dawn of July 2 came with a "clear, red sunrise [that] indicated intense heat...as the day advanced the indications were verified." At about 7:00 a.m., the exhausted survivors of the Northern loss on July 1 received some much needed relief.[4]

Led by Major General Winfield S. Hancock, the Union Second Corps had covered some ninety-two miles the previous week in their pursuit of Lee's Army, covering thirty-two miles on June 29 alone. On crossing the Mason-Dixon Line, however, the tired units marched proudly into Pennsylvania, unfurling their flags over Northern soil instead of the torn landscape of Virginia. When Hancock's men left their overnight camps east of Round Top that morning, the mist still "hung thick and heavy over the ground"; following the stone-fenced Taneytown Road, the column passed Meade's headquarters at the Leister farm on the east face of Cemetery Ridge.

"A few rods further on we turned off from the road to the left," wrote a member of the 14th Connecticut regiment,

And after going up a little ascent, the brigade was halted in column by regiments on a grassy field or plateau of considerable size. In front of and a little to the right on slightly higher ground was a cemetery, on the further edge of which pieces of artillery were planted... Immediately in front of us, when the mist had lifted, we could see across the plain the distant spires and houses of Gettysburg. [5]

Meade's headquarters at the Leister Farm. Ziegler's Grove is visible at the upper left (LC)

Where the northern end of the ridge joined Cemetery Hill, the 3,500-man division of Brigadier General Alexander Hays now faced the small woodlot known as Ziegler's Grove. Initially arrayed in columns by regiment, Colonel Thomas Smyth's brigade faced west from the grove itself, supporting the six smoothbore cannon of Woodruff's Battery I, 1st U.S. Artillery; where the Taneytown Road crested the hill, Colonel Samuel Carroll's small brigade faced north to connect with the Eleventh Corps on the height to the east; and on the slope behind the grove, Colonel George Willard's large New York brigade stood in support. Along the ridge to the south, Hancock placed his other divisions under Brigadier Generals John Gibbon and John Caldwell – some 6,900 men; Hancock reinforced the ridgeline position with twenty-four more cannon, and deployed a company of Massachusetts Sharpshooters to counter any probes from the fields to the west. [6]

STOP 2: CEMETERY RIDGE - THE BRIAN FARM
Leave your vehicle and walk west through the trees of Ziegler's Grove until you reach Hancock Avenue and the Brian Farm on the crest of Cemetery Ridge (see Map 1). Stop by the monument and cannon marking the position of Woodruff's Battery I, 1st U.S. Artillery.
** CAUTION: Avoid walking on the pavement of Hancock Avenue – traffic approaching from the left has limited visibility.

At the foot of the western slope, the Emmitsburg Road enters modern Gettysburg (where the road is now known as Steinwehr Avenue). To your left front, the extension of Long Lane intersects the road, and marks the boundary of the National Military Park in this area. Obviously much has changed in this section of the National Park; to understand the struggle for the Bliss Farm, one needs to envision how different this area looked in 1863.

At the time of the battle, this part of Long Lane did not exist (however, much of the original north-south path of Long Lane is still extant beyond the homes to the west). The fields to your left (south) were fenced much as they are today, but contained a variety of crops and pastureland. Where modern commercial and residential development stands north of the lane, acres of similarly cultivated fields once stretched almost a mile up the valley to the original south edge of Gettysburg. Beyond these fields, the imposing

Lutheran Theological Seminary would be visible across the valley, crowning the northern end of the wooded ridge that bears its name.

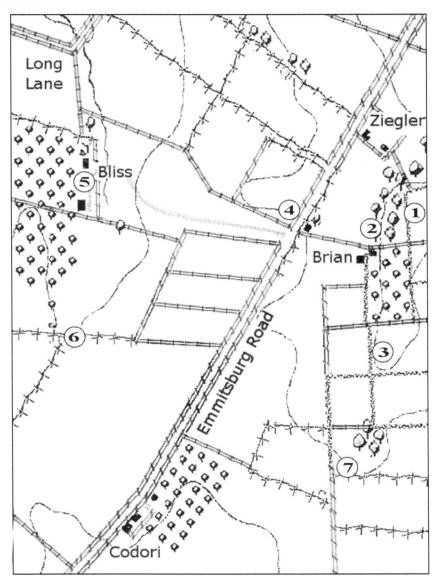

Map 2: Tour Stops

Brian farmhouse as it appeared shortly after the battle (LC)

In 1863, the buildings to your left were home to Abraham Brian, his wife, and five children. One of Gettysburg's African-American residents, Brian owned the approximately twenty-acre farm here, including property on the east side of the ridge, the orchard south of the house, and a tenant building by the Emmitsburg Road. Beside the barn, the section of stone wall and the white fence extending down the slope mark Brian's farm lane.

When you are ready, proceed along the sidewalk to your left past the Brian farmhouse and stop on the south side. As described in the previous section, Hancock's Corps eventually occupied Cemetery Ridge from Ziegler's Grove to the large domed Pennsylvania monument visible to the south. Stay in this area for the following section.

Awaiting orders under a nearby oak, Captain Samuel Fiske of the 14th Connecticut studied the same valley more critically:

> We are drawn up in a fine position, on elevated ground overlooking a valley and meadow. The enemy occupying, we suppose, a somewhat similar position on the other side of said valley.... We seem to be a little in doubt whether the enemy is seeking to entice us into the valley to take us at disadvantage, or whether he is just withdrawing himself entirely, and keeping up the firing in a small way to cover his retreat.

Almost prophetically, Fiske added: "Perhaps it will be as well to wait the issue of events quietly. Very likely the butternuts will burst out upon us at sundown, after the old Jackson style, with the heaviest kind of attack, which will give us all we can wish for…"[8]

As his brigades settled around Ziegler's Grove, Hays sent skirmishers from the 1st Delaware, and the 111th and 125th New York into the valley to test the intentions of that enemy. For, as one New Yorkers recalled, "As the morning lengthened, in the distance among some brush behind a fence, men were seen moving into positions as skirmishers.", *(See Appendix A for more information on skirmishing).*[9]

The gray-clad figures advancing into the mist-shrouded fields across the valley were members of Brigadier General Alfred M. Scales' North Carolina infantry brigade. At dawn, the depleted unit had been sent to extend the Confederate army's right flank on Seminary Ridge. Seriously weakened in the first day's fighting, the brigade's remaining 500 men were led that morning by their only unwounded field officer, Colonel William Lowrance. Ordered to hold the position "at all hazards," Lowrance later wrote, "I considered it *hazardous* in the extreme considering our weakness in numbers and the importance of the position. I threw out a strong line of skirmishers extending fully one half mile to the right, inclining to the rear." The morning's humid calm gave way to gunfire as the Rebel line put up stiff opposition to the Union advance.[10]

Brigadier General Alexander Hays (LC)

As the day brightened, more detachments of Hays' division advanced through the still tall stands of grain, but the stubborn Southern line pressed them back again. It was clear the see-saw action would become the template for the struggle; as one Union officer noted:

> *We send a line of skirmishers down into the meadow among the grass and wheat fields. The enemy push out a rather stronger line from their position, and crowd our boys back. We put in a few more companies, and force them to a retrograde movement; and so the line wavers to and fro.* [11]

Watching from Cemetery Ridge, Brigadier General Alexander Hays was well suited to the pattern of challenge that was developing. Born near Pittsburgh, Hays graduated from West Point in 1844 in the lower half of his class (as did Ulysses Grant, Hays' close friend who graduated the year previous) and served with distinction in the Mexican War. On reentering the Army in 1861, his bold style led to series of promotions. After being seriously wounded at Second Manassas, Hays rose to the rank of brigadier general, eventually succeeding to division command only three days before Gettysburg. On July 2, 1863, Alexander Hays was a few days short of 44 years old, a hard-living, fiery leader ready to defend his home state. At Gettysburg, Hays' aggressive leadership would see three horses shot from under him, and all but two of his fifteen aides become casualties; this grim recognition was yet to come.[12]

In response to the Southern advance, at about 10:00 a.m. Hays ordered all of Willard's 39th New York regiment to reinforce the skirmish line in his front. Crossing the fence-lined Emmitsburg Road, the 269-man unit fanned out into the fields north of the Bliss buildings. Known as the "Garibaldi Guard," the 39th was mobilized in 1861 entirely of European immigrants. The unit would have a checkered career, becoming part of the 12,000, "Harper's Ferry Boys," forced to surrender to Stonewall Jackson in 1862; sent to a parole camp, their enthusiasm festered. The following January, the regiment became part of Hays' first brigade command, and under his firm hand, the unit had been totally revamped in the months before Gettysburg.[13]

That warm July morning, Hays could see the New Yorkers' skirmish line was already in trouble. Additions to the stubborn Rebel detachment had moved into the orchard west of the Bliss barn, and the flank of the 39th N.Y. began to unravel. Trailing aides and the banner bearing the Third Division's blue trefoil, the willful Hays rode out to the skirmish line – in the meadow 600 yards to the west – shouting instructions and encouragement. As described by Colonel Clinton MacDougall of the 111th New York, "It was the first and last time I ever saw a division commander with flag and staff on the skirmish line, an act of superb gallantry…"

As a result, the Northern skirmish line stabilized; after four hours under Rebel guns in the intense mid-day heat, the 39th New York was withdrawn, having lost twenty-eight of their number. [14]

14th Connecticut monument circa 1880 (Page-14th CT)

STOP 3: 14TH CONNECTICUT MONUMENT
When it is safe, cross Hancock Avenue and follow the stone wall past the monuments marking the positions of the 111th New York of Willard's Brigade, and the 12th New Jersey, 1st

Delaware, and 14th Connecticut of Smyth's Brigade; all of these units saw action on the Bliss Farm. Stop by the Connecticut monument and face west. The monument here was erected in 1885 and this wall marks the line taken by the Connecticut regiment later on July 2. Beyond the Emmitsburg Road, and about 600 yards to your right front, look for a grassy mound, orchard, and two small monuments midway across the valley (foliage permitting). These mark the site of the William Bliss Farm. For the following section, you may remain at the wall by the Connecticut marker.

As the sharpshooting intensified between the opposing lines, shelter became a scarce commodity. One participant, Sergeant E.B. Tyler of the 14th Connecticut, later recalled:

> *Those of us detailed to go out on the line crawled out across the wheatfield to the fence beyond and lying upon the ground behind the rails began the sharpshooters drill. . . The space between us and the rebel skirmish line was open and clear…and the least showing of head, hand or foot was an invitation for a target of the same. One thing we learned was that the puff of smoke from our rifles made an unpleasantly close target even when we were unseen ourselves.* [15]

Not surprisingly, as the only substantial shelter in the open fields below town, the barn and farmhouse of William Bliss were rapidly becoming the focus of the contest. The Confederate skirmishers were quick to take advantage of the stout brick and stone barn. Entering through the large doors facing their lines, Rebel marksmen soon filled the upper story of the barn, "whence they picked off our men with impunity from the loop-holed windows." In response, Hays dispatched three companies of the 126th New York to clear out the sniper's nest. By midday, a Yankee sortie led by Captain Charles Wheeler was finally successful, capturing the barn and several of the Southern sharpshooters; Wheeler's luck had run out however: by the end of the battle, the skirmishing in this area cost him his life.[16]

JULY 2 – *Afternoon*

Across the valley at the Seminary, Robert E. Lee also watched the growing conflict, devising a strategy he hoped would finish off Meade's Army of the Potomac. The plan called for fresh troops of A.P. Hill's Corps to extend the Rebel flank down Seminary Ridge; 14,000 more fresh troops of James Longstreet's Corps were to march south behind Hill's position on the ridge, turn, and attack the Union line end-on. Supported by Ewell's Corps threatening the Union right at Culp's Hill, Longstreet's men would be joined by Hill's brigades as the attack rolled north. [17]

After holding the flank since dawn, Lowrance's weary Southern brigade was finally relieved by a 7,000 man division under Major Genera R.H. Anderson. In support of a rapidly growing line of artillery, Anderson placed his five fresh brigades along the ridge from the McMillan Farm to Spangler's Woods almost a mile to the south. Formerly a division commander under Longstreet, Richard Anderson was well-liked and had proven himself in previous campaigns to be "brave, prudent, and intelligent." Perhaps too prudent--for some felt that Anderson was not aggressive enough, and that "Longstreet only could elicit his full powers." Without Longstreet's firm hand, Anderson's command style would suffer under Hill's casual direction that afternoon. [18]

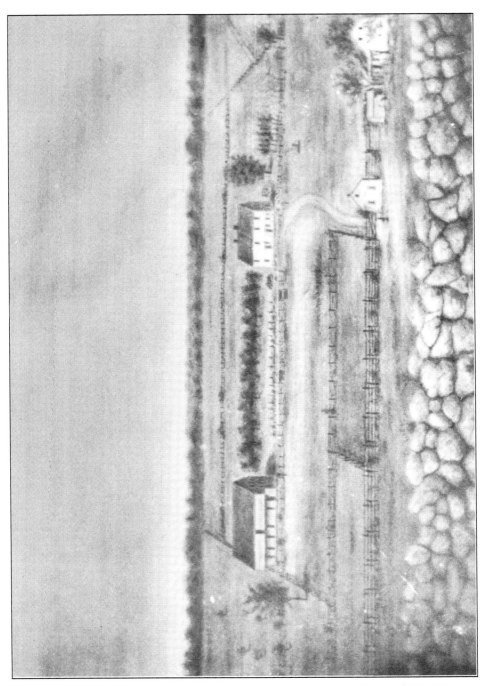

Bliss Farm as it appeared in 1863 – see Image Notes (GNMP)

Major General R.H. Anderson (B&L)   Brigadier General Carnot Posey (LC)

View looking southwest from the Soldiers National Cemetery in 1869. Note the banked section of the Emmitsburg Road visible along the fence at right center The Bliss orchard still stands in the right distance. (WAF)

Facing the Bliss property were 1,300 Mississippians under Brigadier General Carnot Posey. An ardent States Rights advocate and veteran of the Mexican War, by age 45, Posey had earned substantial praise in service to the Confederacy. One of the 48th Mississippi later wrote: "[We were] stationed in support of a battery occupying a slight elevation in our front...beyond the guns, in a wheat field, stood a red barn." As Posey's men occupied the ridge, skirmishers from the 16th and 19th Mississippi advanced to a fence line about 250 yards from the farm buildings and the dispute continued. As recalled by one, "Day very hot and we are much exposed." [19]

STOP 4: EMMITSBURG ROAD & LONG LANE

Retrace your steps back up Hancock Avenue past the Brian barn and turn left down the lane; as you walk, remember that this seemingly insignificant lane was the path of advance for hundreds of Federals deploying to the Bliss Farm.

In 1863, post and rail fences bordered the Emmitsburg Road much as they do today, however, the dirt roadbed was narrower and sunken in some areas. As described earlier, other than Brian's small tenant house beside the lane, and the wood-framed buildings of the Ziegler farm about 300 yards to the north, there was little cover. As described below, the sunken roadbed was a welcome respite for the reserves of the Union skirmish line.

** CAUTION: <u>Traffic may be heavy at the Emmitsburg Road</u>. When it is safe to do so, cross the Road; stop well away from the pavement for the following.

The experience of the Connecticut skirmishers from the west of Cemetery Ridge was typical of the growing conflict around the Bliss Farm:

Our reserve was in the Emmitsburg Road in front of the regiment. The road was sunken nearly two feet, affording some protection at the fence. The picket line was at a fence some 200 yards in advance, and the line of rebel pickets about the same distance further on, some of it by the trees of the Bliss orchard. Our men lay flat upon the ground by the fence hidden and somewhat protected by the posts and the lowest rails. [20]

By 2:00 pm, the temperature had risen to eighty-one degrees, and the sun "bore down with a sweltering, withering effect...." The morning's tentative probes had given way to large-scale maneuvers. In a grand, but unauthorized move, Major General Daniel Sickles was advancing his Union Third Corps to the Emmitsburg Road; by mid-afternoon, the high ground about a mile south of the Bliss property was now occupied by some 10,000 Federals. Embroiled in their flank march behind Seminary Ridge, Longstreet's two Gray divisions were unknowingly headed for the same high ground. With the combatants closing on each other, the conflict intensified all along the line.[21]

North of Long Lane stands the monument the 8th Ohio regiment and, further on, interpretive markers; you may wish to read these before continuing.

According to one contemporary image (page 25), a farm lane intersected the Emmitsburg Road a few yards south of the wooden fence line here, and followed a curving path out to the Bliss property.

PATH A: If you wish to follow this route to the Bliss Farm, turn left down the Emmitsburg Road to the next east-west fence; follow the fence line toward the Bliss Farm; you will rejoin the tour by Stevens Run near the farm site.

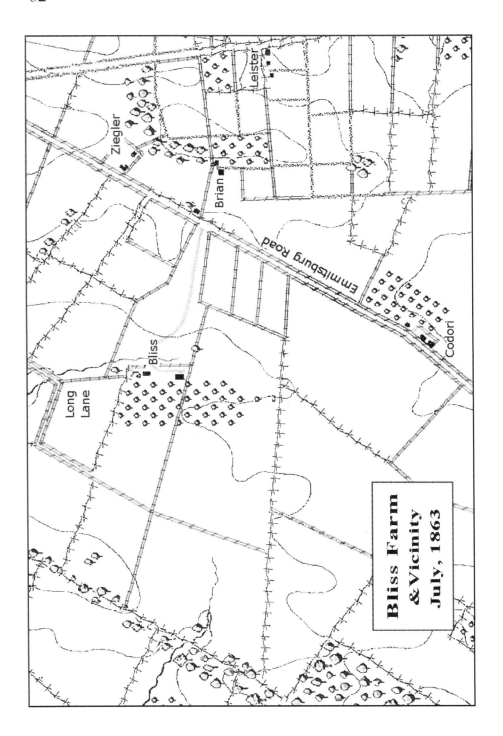

PATH B: To follow Long Lane to the Bliss site, walk west following the NPS fence on the left side of the road. Just past the intersection with modern Highland Avenue on your right, the reconstructed fence turns south across Park property. Stop here and take note of the terrain: the ground behind you rises steadily up to Cemetery Ridge, and forms a broad plateau to the north. This rise offered cover to Southerner skirmishers in this area, but would also obscure the approach of Northern forces to the Bliss Farm.

View southwest toward Bliss Farm as seen from modern Long Lane. The fenceline in the foreground marks Stevens Run; the barn bank is visible at left, and the house foundation pit at right.

STOP 5: THE BLISS FARM
In the meadow beyond the end of the fence, look for a mowed path that leads southwest toward the Bliss site. Follow the path about 75 yards across the field to Stevens Run, the small stream marked by the low ground and scrub. (Note: If the path is not mowed when you visit, please make

your way across the field <u>before</u> the post and rail fence at the end of Long Lane; please respect local residents by not crossing private property).
(PATH A & B rejoin here)
Carefully cross Stevens Run at the gap in the fence and walk up the slope toward the 14th Connecticut marker. In 1863, this area was William Bliss' farmyard. Note that Seminary Ridge and Cemetery Ridge both lie about 600 yards in either direction from this small rise.

One of the combatants later noted, "Mr. Bliss was like many other farmers who give more attention to the architecture and pretentiousness of their barns than they do to their houses." Fortunately, the chaplain of the 14th Connecticut, Henry S. Stevens, later described the buildings in some detail:

> *In front of our skirmish line were two buildings...one was a large barn almost a citadel in itself, It was expensively and elaborately built structure, as barns go, 75 feet long and 33 feet wide, its lower story, or basement, 10 feet high, constructed of stone, and its upper part, 16 feet to the eaves, of bricks, the wall being carried to the gables. Within was an oak frame sufficiently heavy for a barn without walls. There was an overhang 10 feet long across the entire front for the shelter of cattle, and the rear was banked to the first floor--whence the name bank barn--furnishing a driveway for loads to that floor. There were 5 doors in the front wall of the basement and 3 windows in each end; several vertical slits in the upper story front and 2 rows of windows in each end.*
>
> *Ninety paces north of [the barn] was the mansion, a frame building, two stories in height. As it had a front of three rooms width and two front doors, and there now remain*

two cellar excavations with a thick wall in between, over which it stood, indicating a length of about 50 feet, we see that the building must have been long and capacious. [22]

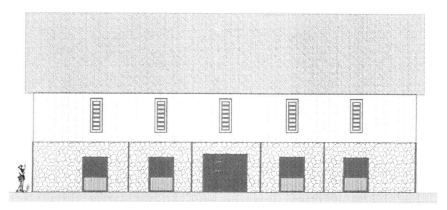

Scale image of the Bliss barn as described by Stevens (eastern face)

The Connecticut and Delaware monuments here mark the house site. As described in Stevens' account, the remaining cellar depression here is only part a much larger foundation.

Now walk west toward the restored orchard and face toward Seminary Ridge. At the time of the battle, farm fields stretched north where modern homes stand today. Just west of the modern homes, the original path of the Long Lane near the Bliss farm is marked by post and rail fences. Remain by the orchard for the following.

At about 4:00 p.m., Longstreet's guns opened, announcing the start of his assault on the Union left. Ezra Simons of 125th New York later penned: "Through the thick smoke the belching of the cannon appeared," the smoke rising, "in huge volumes like heavy summer clouds, enveloping the combatants and obscuring the sun." The light southerly breeze did little to dispel the dark clouds as more Confederate batteries joined to duel with the Union line.

Under the arcing shot and shell, responsibility for the Bliss property had fallen largely to about 290 skirmishers from Hays' Second Brigade, commanded by Colonel Thomas Smyth. Relieving Willard's New Yorkers at the farm, the 1st Delaware and Company I of the 12th New Jersey advanced through the Bliss yard to a fence beyond the barn. Crouching by a fence near the house, Captain Henry Chew and Sergeant Henry Bowen of the 12th New Jersey watched as W.J. Pegram's batteries hammered the Union line on Cemetery Ridge. Bowen recalled, "Evidently the point of direction was the house, as such shot that did not pass over us struck in front of us, they appeared to be on exact line with us." When the sergeant recommended that they move to a more secure spot, Captain Chew stoically explained, "We are as safe here as anywhere, you can't run away from them things." That said, a piece of solid shot tore through the fence by their heads, and the pair promptly moved to the barn.[23]

As the roar of battle to the south rose, Chew discovered that Posey was steadily reinforcing his skirmish line, "so that our attention would not be attracted until they had enough men to drive us away from the barn." Reporting his observations to Lieutenant Colonel Edward Harris of the 1st Delaware, Chew suggested they report the build-up and ask for reinforcements. The New Jersey captain was curtly informed that Harris "understood his business," and would make his own decisions. Chew returned to his men and awaited the attack that he was sure would follow.[24]

Chew was not far from the mark: by this point, Posey had committed the balance of the 19th and 48th Mississippi--almost 700 men--to his skirmish line around the farm. Posey next committed another 385 rifles of the 16th Mississippi to reinforce that line. With the pressure from almost 1,000 Mississippians, it is not surprising that Sergeant Bowen recalled that the "firing had become very hot, [and] in a few minutes it assumed almost the character of a battle." Captain George Price of the 1st Delaware agreed, "a line of battle...advanced against us; their skirmish line was absorbed by [it] as they came upon them."[25]

The growing pressure on both front and flank, as well as the unnerving Southern assault to the south took their toll on the thin Blue skirmish line. The report for the 1st Delaware states tersely, "At 4 p.m. the ammunition of the men being exhausted, Lieutant Colonel Harris withdrew the right wing of the regiment." With the retreat of the Delaware flank, the whole line faced collapse. As Sergeant Bowen recalled, the withdrawal was hardly ceremonious:

> *Looking around I saw the men of the 1st Delaware running to the rear...I out and took after them, soon catching up with Lieut. Col. Harris of the 1st Del. who was getting to the rear as fast as he could, he swung his sword around, called me a hard name, telling me to go back, this I did not do but made a detour around him and got across that 3/4 of a mile in record time.*

Upon his return to Cemetery Ridge, the winded Harris was likely on the receiving end of a "hard name" from an angry Major General Hancock, who promptly placed him under arrest for the unauthorized withdrawal.[26]

Driving out the remaining pockets of Yanks at the farm, Posey's men moved into the buildings and "busied themselves with picking off our battery men, officers and skirmishers." In the fields to the south of the barn, the skirmish line of the 106th Pennsylvania began to waver under the flank fire from the Mississippians. Assuming the barn was occupied by a few Southerners, Captain James Lynch led the skirmish reserve of the Pennsylvania regiment-- perhaps 25 men--to retake the buildings; the Southerners allowed the Northerners to get into the yard before demanding their surrender. Under fire, Lynch and his company retreated, losing another twelve men before they could get out of range.[27]

Now walk about fifty yards south to the markers for the 12th New Jersey and 14th Connecticut that mark the barn site. The earthen mound is what remains of the ramp leading into a typical Pennsylvania "bank barn," allowing grain storage on the second floor as well as easy access to supply the stalls below. If you wish, take some time to explore this area, but please help preserve resources by not climbing on this bank.

When you are ready, remain in the fenced barnyard and face toward Cemetery Ridge for the following.

The 14th Connecticut marker at the barn site after dedication in 1885. Note the still-standing orchard trees. (Page-14th CT)

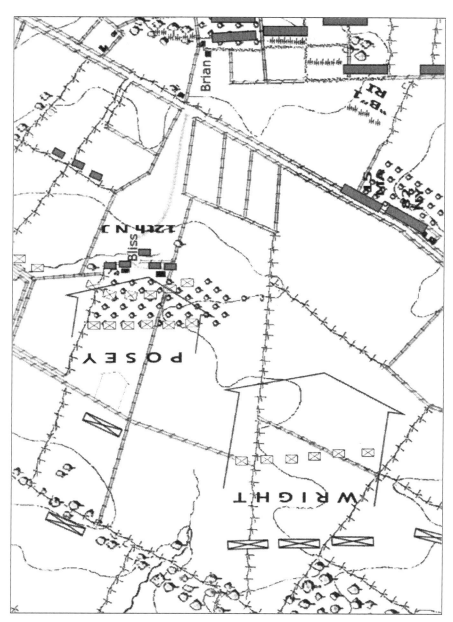

Map 4: Situation around Bliss Farm - approx.6:30 pm

Headquartered at the Brian house on the ridge, Brigadier General Hays and his staff had also gained the attention of the Mississippi riflemen. At 5:00 p.m., Hays ordered Colonel Smyth to seize the Bliss buildings and reestablish the skirmish line there. Observed by "many 'Yanks' on one side, and soon the object of interest to the 'Rebs' on the other," 150 volunteers from the 12th New Jersey under Captain Samuel Jobes crossed the fences at the Emmitsburg Road and moved "by company into line."[28]

Raising a cheer, the four New Jersey companies shouldered their smoothbore muskets and double-quicked across the 400 yards to the Bliss buildings. Immediately Posey's sharpshooters and A.P. Hill's batteries opened fire on the charging Blue line, "raking us awfully," recalled a New Jersey soldier, "dropping men to the right and to the left." Upon reaching the farmyard, the New Jersey column halted, delivered a volley of "buck and ball" into the barn; surrounding the building, the New Jersey detachment captured scores of the Mississippians.[29]

The balance of Posey's line was intact however, and continued sharpshooting from the Bliss house, just 75 yards away. One of Jobes' companies promptly charged the Bliss house, and brought the detachment's catch to 92 of Posey's men, including seven officers. But with the sounds of the Third Corps struggle rumbling up the valley from the south, the New Jersey tenure of the Bliss farm was almost over.[30]

By this time, Longstreet's assault was well under way and rolling north. The en echelon advance initiated by over 14,000 of Longstreet's veterans had broken the Union left flank at Devil's Den, pushed through Sickles' salient at the Peach Orchard, and unhinged the advanced Union line at the Emmitsburg Road. As planned, Anderson's division of A.P. Hill's Corps was to take up the attack next, progressing northward through the brigades of Wilcox, Lang, Wright,

Posey, and Mahone, each hammering the Federal line in their front. At about 6:30 p.m., observing the Southern advance on their right, 1,400 Georgians under Brig. Gen. Ambrose R. Wright were set to begin their drive across the valley.[31]

Brigadier General Ambrose Wright (LC)

A few hundred yards away, the four New Jersey companies holding the Bliss buildings were in a tight spot. Reestablishing the skirmish line at the farm had already cost the Blue detachment forty-two of their number. Despite their initial success in seizing the buildings, a brief look through any window would confirm their precarious position. Just west of the farm, several hundred of Posey's men still held the area around the Bliss orchard. At 6:00 p.m., a strong line of skirmishers from Pender's division appeared in Long Lane only 250 yards to the north, threatening the New Jersey flank. Now to the south, skirmishers from the 2nd Georgia Battalion were driving the Union line there, clearing the way for Wright's advance. The combination of these threats was doubtless sufficient reason to clear out. Discreetly, but to resounding cheers, the Blue-coated companies withdrew to Cemetery Ridge with their captives.[32]

STOP 6: WRIGHT'S ADVANCE
The tour will now return to Cemetery Ridge by following the Park trail that parallels the Confederate advance. Locate the trail by looking across the orchard to the southeast; locate the Codori Barn and beyond, the crest of Big Round Top. Between them, and about 275 yards away, is a break in the post and rail fence that marks the trail.
Leave the farmyard and walk southeast through the orchard to this fence opening. Stop there on the trail for the following.

By 7:00 p.m., the Federal positions on Cemetery Ridge had changed dramatically. Well over a third of Hancock's Corps had been sent south to reinforce Sickles' collapsing line: Caldwell's entire division had been sent into the carnage at the Wheatfield, while one of Hays' brigades and almost half of Gibbon's division were parceled out to shore up other sections of the Third Corps position. Supporting Cushing's battery (A, 4th U.S.), Gibbon's remaining regiments held the area around the small grove of oak trees south of Hays' line. In front of Gibbon's position, only two regiments and one battery held the 600 yard gap between Sickles' dangling right flank on the Emmitsburg Road and the balance of the Second Corps line atop Cemetery Ridge. Starting their advance according to plan, Wright's Confederates were headed straight for that gap.[33]

Stepping off Seminary Ridge to the left of Wilcox's and Lang's advancing infantry, Wright's 3rd, 22nd, and 48th Georgia were greeted with a "terrific fire of shells into our ranks." Absorbing the skirmishers of the 2nd Georgia, the Southern battle line moved rapidly across the fields, taking advantage of the cover in slight hollows in the field to pause and reform. Coming within musket range of the advanced Union line, Wright later recalled, "We were in a hot place, and looking to my left through the smoke, I perceived that neither Posey nor Mahone had advanced, and that my left was totally unprotected." Wright immediately dispatched an aide to Major General Anderson, who replied that both brigades, "had been ordered in and that he would reiterate the order."[34]

Unfortunately, something had gone amiss in Anderson's orders to the left wing of his division. The breakdown in communication that would plague Robert E. Lee's plans that afternoon came to the fore: while Anderson later wrote that each of his brigades was ordered to advance in turn, Brigadier General Posey claimed that his last orders were to advance, "but two of my regiments, and deploy them closely as skirmishers." The resulting gradual deployment of Posey's men to the Bliss property that afternoon had removed the Yankee threat, but the sustained action and resulting casualties had also destroyed the Mississippians ability to move as a cohesive fighting unit. As Wright's line swept past the Bliss yard, only Posey's 48th Mississippi and part of the 19th Mississippi moved forward on the Georgia brigade's flank.[35]

Using the fenced path, now follow the advance toward Cemetery Ridge; note the slight rises in the ground that covered much of Wright's Brigade from direct fire from the Union line.

When you reach the fence on the Emmitsburg Road, <u>do not cross here</u>; instead, turn right and proceed to the next *fence opening about 100 yards further south near the Codori house. Stop at this opening and face toward Cemetery Ridge for the following.*

Firing rapidly from a makeshift breastwork of fence rails just east of the Emmitsburg Road, the 600 men of Gibbon's 82nd New York and 15th Massachusetts only partially filled the gap in the Union line north of the Codori buildings. On a small rise behind the advanced line, the six Napoleons of Brown's battery (B, 1st R.I.) showered the converging Gray line with spherical case shot and, as they grew closer, double canister. Undaunted, Wright's battle line "would waver for a moment, then close up and continue forward."[36]

Modern view looks east toward Cemetery Ridge where Wright's Brigade crossed the Emmitsburg Road. Monument for the 15th Massachusetts is at right; Brown's Battery occupied the brushy knoll at left center.

In the Codori yard to your front and right are the monuments for the 15th Massachusetts and 82nd New York, the regiments who faced the onslaught by Wright's Brigade. Up the slope beyond, you can see the bushy rise in front of the Union line that marks the advance position held by Brown's Rhode Island artillery.

STOP 7: BREAKTHROUGH
** CAUTION: <u>Traffic may be heavy at the Emmitsburg Road</u>; when it is safe to do so, cross the Road.
To follow the advance, pass through the fence opening north of the Codori yard and keep the snake-rail fence on your right as you proceed to Cemetery Ridge. Just past the knoll that marks Brown's Battery, turn left (north) to follow the trail toward a bench and the marker for Wright's Brigade. Note the shelves of rock in this area that are likely those mentioned in Wright's accounts. Follow the path beyond the marker to the location of "Brown's Gate," where the Rhode Island guns retreated to the Union line.
Stop where the trail crosses onto Cemetery Ridge and face toward the Codori Farm for the following.

In their accounts, both Gibbon and Wright would come to describe the Confederate charge with the same term--impetuous --suggesting a brief or furious action; the advance from the Emmitsburg Road up the slope was undoubtedly both. Charging out of the thick smoke billowing over the field, the long Rebel line flanked one, then both of the Union regiments at the Codori yard. With both colonels and almost half their number shot down, the two Blue units fell back up the slope in disarray.

To the north, marksmen from Posey's 19th Mississippi advanced to within sixty yards of the Rhode Island guns, driving the artillerymen from their pieces three different times. Ordered to limber up in the growing hail of lead, drivers struggled to pull the guns away even as the battery's horses collapsed in their traces. Although unable to bring off two of the guns, the rest of the New Englanders escaped up the slope through a gap in the stone wall.[37]

Modern view of Cemetery Ridge and "Brown's Gate"; Wright's men attempted to seize Union cannon jammed at this wall.

As the left regiments of Wright's brigade claimed the prized Napoleons, the balance of the Second Corps line atop the ridge raked their column with canister and small arms fire. Sweeping past the struggle on their left, the right wing of the Georgia brigade cleared the Codori buildings with less resistance, and advanced with their line relatively intact. Charging up the slope, "in line, in column, and in masses which are neither, with yells, and thick volleys," the Georgia troops swarmed toward Gibbon's thin line behind the wall atop the ridge--and the wide gap on Gibbon's left.[38]

Crossing the stone wall south of the copse of trees, "the head of [the Rebel] column," Brigadier General Gibbon remembered, "came quite through a vacancy in our line to the left of my division." There the Georgians again found Brown's hapless battery, and as an officer of the 7th Michigan witnessed, "they succeeded in passing through the guns of the battery on our left, driving the gunners from their posts. The line on our left gave way, and our flank was almost turned." A Gray color bearer planted his banner on one of the abandoned guns, and the jubilant Rebel line pierced the Union line on Cemetery Ridge.[39]

"We were now complete masters of the field," Wright glowingly recalled, "having gained the key ... of the enemy's whole line." But Wright's isolated spearhead was still without support on either flank. Lacking reinforcements, Wilcox's and Lang's brigades had been stalled at the foot of the slope to the south and were forced to withdraw. Back at the Bliss farm, a perplexed Carnot Posey held back his last regiment, waiting in the fading light for support from William Mahone's brigade. Inexplicably, despite entreaties from Posey and orders from Anderson himself, Brigadier General Mahone insisted he was ordered only to support Pegram's artillery, and his brigade never budged from Seminary Ridge.[40]

The Northern forces were quick to take advantage of Wright's exposed position. As Gibbon's men around the copse poured volleys into the surging Gray line, columns of the 13th Vermont and 106th Pennsylvania charged around Wright's unprotected flanks. Unsupported, their onslaught blunted, the Southerners, "halted, wavered, and fell back," into the gathering dusk. Reforming in the fields to the west,

Wright was pained to find only about half of his brigade had returned from their foray onto Cemetery Ridge.[41]

Across the valley, Hancock had no sooner reformed the Second Corps line along the ridge, when the uproar of a new assault came from the Union right. Hancock quickly dispatched Hays' reserve brigade under Colonel Samuel S. Carroll, followed by the exhausted 71st and 106th Pennsylvania from Gibbon's line. The timely arrival of Carroll's men on East Cemetery Hill would help break the Rebel foothold there and secure the Union line.[42]

If you wish, take a moment to study this position. Note that Cemetery Ridge is relatively low in this area. It should come as no surprise that two Southern assaults – one that briefly broke through the Union line here on July 2, and Robert E. Lee's final assault on July 3 – would strike the same area.

When you are ready, follow Hancock Avenue north, and return to the 14th Connecticut monument for the following section.

Regretting his lost opportunity on July 2, Wright would later pen an overzealous, if not somewhat imaginative report of his brigade's actions. "I have not the slightest doubt," he asserted, "that I should have been able to have maintained my position on the heights ... if there had been a protecting force on my left, or if the brigade on my right had not been forced to retire." Undoubtedly, the assault lacked much of the coordination necessary for success. However, some of Wright's foes maintained the source of his failure lay on William Bliss' doorstep. Joseph Ward of the 106th Pennsylvania claimed that, "had Posey's brigade not been checked at the Bliss house, he would have been supporting Wright." Lieutenant William Potter of the 12th New Jersey agreed:

> *Every brigade from Lee's right up to Posey's brigade advanced that afternoon. Of Posey's brigade, the 16th Mississippi was posted in the Bliss barn and was captured practically as a whole. No advance was made by Posey's brigade nor by any of Hill's brigade's to Posey's left upon that day. If these remaining brigades had advanced, we should have had need of all of our troops upon our front and Carroll and the 106th Pennsylvania could not have been spared [to secure Cemetery Hill].*[43]

But the time for a concerted Southern effort was long past. As his scattered units reorganized at the Bliss farm after Wright's repulse, Posey and Colonel W.H. Taylor of the 12th Mississippi did their best to reform the brigade in the dark. Ordered back to Seminary Ridge, Posey left Taylor with his Mississippians to picket the now still Bliss property, and again formed his brigade behind the ridge. *(See Appendix B for further discussion of Wright's Breakthrough)* [44]

JULY 3 – *Morning*

Dawn of July 3, "broke clear and cloudless." Replacing the night's picket line, companies B and D of 14th Connecticut moved into the fields across the Emmitsburg Road. One member of Company B, Sergeant E.B. Tyler wrote:

> *We were stationed two or three fence lengths apart and although we could hardly see each other, for previous to Pickett's charge the standing grain afforded considerable protection from view, we occasionally spoke to each other for companionship or to ascertain if each was all right.*

Tyler noted that one comrade, Samuel Huxham, didn't reply: he was later found beside the fence – a bullet through his head. Huxham had, "risen up to a kneeling position and was aiming through the middle fence rails...the very one that attracted [his] attention was the one that proved too quick for him... [45]

As the day brightened, the "zip" of Rebel lead among the Union batteries atop the ridge made it clear the Bliss buildings were still held by Gray marksmen. By 9:00 a.m., Colonel Smyth had ordered the sharpshooter's nest cleaned out again. Led by Captain Richard Thompson, the other five companies of the 12th New Jersey (F,A,D,C,K) filed down the Brian farm lane to the Emmitsburg Road. Sergeant H. M. Avis of Co. F, later noted:

I was an active participant in one of those charges and a warmly-interested eyewitness to the other one... I am free to say that I enjoyed watching the first far more than I did participating in the second.

To minimize their losses, the 200-man detachment stayed in column instead of deploying "by battalion into line," and charged across the meadow at the double-quick. The formation presented a narrower front to the enemy marksmen, but the front of the column, Company F, suffered the consequences. As the company crested the small rise midway to the buildings, the concentrated Rebel fire killed three and wounded several others in the front of the column.[46]

Reaching the buildings, the New Jersey troops charged into the barn and found all but three of the Southern tenants gone. Learning from their losses the previous day, the Mississippians escaped down the bank in the rear of the barn and resumed firing from the orchard beyond. Sergeant Frank Riley of Co. K recalled:

> *I can see them running until reaching a respectable distance, they halted and commenced skirmishing. I with some few others mounted the steps leading to the mow, it was here we found one rebel. We thrust our bayonets into the hay – exploring - but to no avail. I remember walking out on a joist, the flooring having been torn away, to a lattice window, looking toward the rebel lines...and saw a reb officer trying to form and move forward a line of skirmishers. While I did the firing from there, others were loading and passing their guns to me.*

As others rushed up to the second story mow, the Gray riflemen shot Company F's Abel Shute through both knees and he lay mortally wounded, just out of reach in the yawning doorway. [47]

Still occupying Long Lane just north of the Bliss buildings, Pender's Southerners were joining the fray. Commanding a brigade of South Carolinians, Colonel Abner Perrin described, "At one time the enemy poured down a perfect torrent of light troops from the hill which swept my skirmishers back upon the main line. I now ordered the Fourteenth [South Carolina] to deploy and charge the enemy." Viewed from Sergeant Riley's perch in the Bliss barn, the 430 Rebels looked even more formidable. "I had fired perhaps a half dozen times when we heard them calling from below, come down! Come down quickly...they are trying to capture us!" And sure enough here to our right could be seen what looked like whole brigade. No Libby for us!"[48]

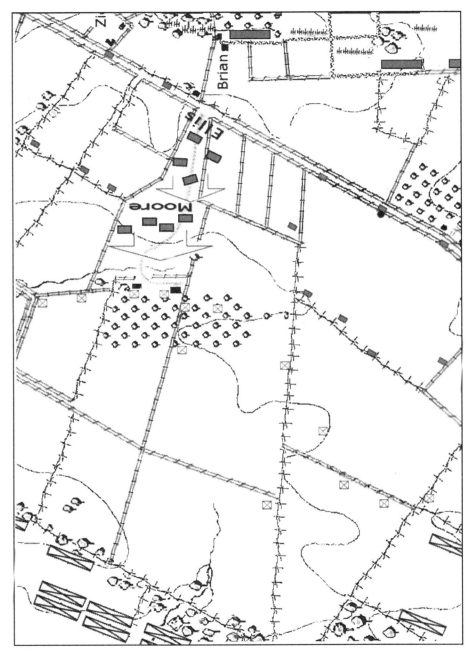

Map 5: Situation at Bliss Farm at approx. 10:00 a.m., July 3: the 14th Connecticut "Scatter and Run"

In the face of mounting pressure from front and flank, punctuated by the bursts of Pegram's artillery fire overhead, the New Jersey companies withdrew from the buildings, gathering their casualties as they fell back. The brief raid on the Bliss farm had netted another five prisoners, but a like number of the New Jersey detachment were dead or dying, and at least twenty-five had been wounded. Before long, silhouetted in the morning sun, the Blue figures atop Cemetery Ridge again filled the sights of the Rebel sharpshooters.[49]

Captain Samuel Moore   Major Theodore Ellis
(Page – 14th CT)   (Page – 14th CT)

Undaunted, Hays ordered yet another sortie. This detail would include four companies--about 60 men--of the depleted 14th Connecticut, who were ordered to occupy the buildings "to stay." Chaplain Stevens later wondered, "Why a force only one half as large as either of the parties previously sent for the same purpose was sent this time is one of the inscrutable things in the varying wisdom of war."[50]

Distracted only by "the hottest sun that ever shone on mortals," and the incessant gunfire from Culp's Hill, eyes on both sides of the valley watched as another Blue column filed down the slope. Led by Captain Samuel Moore of Company F, the detachment began to move out in compact formation, when, from the ridge behind them, they heard Brigadier General. Hays bellow, "Scatter and run!" Crossing the Emmitsburg Road, the Connecticut companies fanned out as they sprinted across the fields. Despite the scattered target, the Confederate riflemen, "now well read in the business," soon found the range and several of the New Englanders fell.[51]

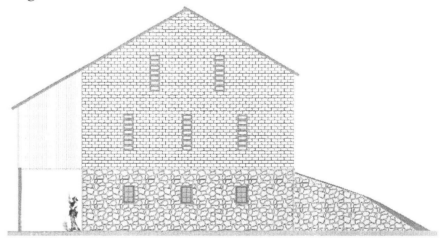

Bliss barn as described by Chaplain Stevens (north face)

"Every man was put to his mettle and ran with all his might," but upon reaching the barn, the winded New Englanders found the Rebels had again disappeared into the farmhouse and orchard, where they resumed firing at close quarters., "[The farmhouse], which had not figured much in former attacks," recalled one Yank, "[was] now becoming quite formidable as a place of offense and defense." Also, the problem faced by others defending the barn now became painfully clear: although the side of the barn facing Cemetery Ridge contained numerous doors and windows, much of the structure facing the Southern lines was occupied by the wide doorway in the second story and the large earthen bank leading up to it. Outnumbered, pinned in the barn by gunfire from three sides, and unable to return any effective fire, the Connecticut detail was in a dire situation. [52]

14th Connecticut marker at the Bliss house site, circa 1891. Note the mature orchard trees beyond (Page-14th CT)

Ordered to break the deadlock, and again seize the "damned white house," Major Theodore Ellis led the remaining four companies of the 14th Connecticut across the Emmitsburg Road. As Ellis' men headed farther north to reach the farmhouse, they were met by a harrowing flank fire from Pender's men in Long Lane. In a telling recollection, Chaplain Stevens described: "The men could never describe their feelings on those mad runs for life. We have never heard any really attempt it. The excitement, the frenzied effort, the terrible sense of imminent, savage danger could not be clearly called up or words express them.[53]

Closing on the farmhouse, the New Englanders traded parting shots with the Rebels, who again headed to the orchard beyond. One veteran recalled, "How cooly [Sergeant] Sam Scranton shot a rebel in the doorway of that troublesome house as if he would have shot a squirrel on his father's farm." Entering by the two front doors, the Connecticut men found the building a poor shelter. With "bullets piercing the thin siding and windows," some of Ellis' men took their chances outside, or ran the gauntlet to the barn.[54]

In response, Pegram's artillery on Seminary Ridge pounded the Bliss buildings with a relentless fire. At a reunion years later, a member of Virginia's Purcell Artillery later told a survivor: "The men were directed to place ten shells beside each of the four guns of the battery and continue firing them leisurely at the buildings until they were vacated. 'And,' said he, 'we fired every one of those shells at you.'" One of the "leisurely" rounds of case-shot hit squarely on the roof of the barn, killing one and wounding another of the Connecticut men on the floor below.[55]

It was barely mid-morning, and the Bliss buildings had been captured three times with little result except the ensnarement of the attackers. "Though the men plied their rifles the best they could, they seemed in a trap and doomed to stay until exterminated, for the order as understood, was to 'take and hold' the buildings." Unbeknownst to the New Englanders, Colonel Smyth had modified their orders. As the last companies left Cemetery Ridge, Company I's Lieutenant Frederick Seymour asked Smyth, "If...the rebs make it so hot we can't hold [the house and barn] shall we fire them?" Colonel Smyth replied, "We don't know the word can't!" Thinking better of his bravado, Smyth added, "If they make it too hot for you, burn the buildings and return to the line." Unfortunately, Semour was shot in the leg as the company crossed the fields, and he, along with Smyth's orders, never reached the buildings. [56]

Recognizing the desperate situation, Brigadier General Hays dispatched Sergeant Charles Hitchcock of the 111th New York to relay the orders to torch the buildings. Armed with cartridge papers and matches, the volunteer made his way across the fields to the barn and relayed his message. With great understatement, Hitchcock later wrote, "I never considered the mere act of setting fire to the buildings as dangerous, but there was considerable risk getting there and back again."[57]

To ensure the order would be delivered, Smyth asked for yet another messenger. Although ill, Smyth's Inspector General, Captain J. Parke Postles of the 1st Delaware volunteered to deliver the orders and promptly set off on horseback. "It was a constant wonder and surprise to me, he recalled, "that none of the bullets, which I heard whistling around and so close to me, had hit me." Realizing if he stopped moving, "they would kill me sure," Postles kept his horse rearing and plunging even as he gave the order to the amazed Connecticut officer at the barn doorway. His duty complete, Postles raced out of the yard. When about 300 yards away, Postles took off his cap, and shook it defiantly at the Rebels; in response, Postles recalled, "[the Southerners] immediately set up a 'rebel yell' and ceased firing at me."[58]

The New Englanders needed no more urging. Upon hearing the order, "wisps of hay and straw were soon on fire and ... applied at different places in the barn, and in the house a straw bed was emptied on the floor and the match applied." Despite the heavy shelling and rifle fire, the Connecticut men took time to bring their dead and wounded comrades back through the gauntlet they had entered but a short time before. 59

Stopping in the relative safety of the Emmitsburg Road, the New Englanders looked back with relief on the Bliss farm, where, "flames...[were] bursting fiercely out of the house and barn." Their relief must have been short-lived as they realized the attack had cost the regiment another 20 of their already diminished number, including three killed or mortally wounded. 60

In just over twenty-four hours, the "skirmishing" for the no-man's land around the Bliss buildings had involved over ten regiments, Union and Confederate, and created hundreds of casualties for both sides. Looking back on the episode at an 1880's reunion, Chaplain Stevens might have spoken for all those involved when he wrote:

"We believe [the fight for the Bliss buildings] to have been the most notable episode connected with the doings of any <u>individual regiment</u> occurring during the great battle of Gettysburg. ... Had the buildings been destroyed the first time captured by our troops, many lives uselessly sacrificed would have been spared and much needless suffering avoided. It was one of the 'fool things' of war. Yet it was a grand lesson to our boys, and it furnished one of the brightest points in their most glowing record. In that sortie some precious lives went out, some cripples were made, and every man that escaped hurt came back panting and

wearied and feeling that "out of the jaws of death he had come." [61]

You may return to the Brian Farm and Ziegler's Grove for the remaining sections.

JULY 3 – Afternoon

By 11:00 a.m., Robert E. Lee's final plan for victory at Gettysburg was solidified; centered on virtually the same spot where Wright's Georgians had briefly succeeded, the attack on Cemetery Ridge would now be made the divisions of Pickett, Pettigrew, and Trimble: some 13,000 men. However, by the time the Confederate advance started at 3:00 p.m., the Bliss farm was no longer a point of contention; the Southerners merely maneuvered around the smoldering ruins en route to their fate on the ridge beyond.

Aftermath

After six years laboring to establish his home, William Bliss would have to start over. Like many Gettysburg property owners, Bliss submitted claims for compensation; initially, his requests amounted to $1,256.08 in lost property; and like other claimants, Bliss' claims also went unanswered. By 1865, with no resolution in sight, the Bliss family could no longer remain in Gettysburg. Their 60-acre property was offered at sale for $3000; considering the post-battle condition of the fields surrounding Gettysburg, it should come as little surprise there was scant interest. That October, Bliss settled for the amount of $1000 from his neighbor, Nicholas Codori. By the end of the year, the family had returned to New York, where Bliss purchased yet another farm in Chatauqua County. [62]

From his new home, Bliss resubmitted his claim for $3,256.05 in compensation: the original $1,256.08 in personal property, plus $1,700 for the destruction of his house and barn, $240 for fencing, and $60 for hay & grain. The family received a preliminary offer of payment from the State of Pennsylvania in 1871, but the offer soon evaporated when forwarded to Federal bureaucracy. The family's claims for compensation were continued through, and after, the couple's death in the 1880's. Finally, in 1902, the last surviving daughter, Frances, received official notice from the Roosevelt administration – they ruled the government was not responsible for damages incurred "during necessary military operations." [63]

In the end, a fitting quote was recorded in the *Gettysburg Star and Banner*. The paper reported:

The old man and his wife and two daughters were turned out with nothing but the clothes they had on. Everything was destroyed by the fire in the buildings, and his fences, cattle and crops were swept away by the battle, leaving with him the bare land which he was obliged to sacrifice in order to support his family. He was utterly ruined, but such was his patriotic love for his country that looking on the wreck of all of his early possessions, he exclaimed, "Let it go; if I had twenty farms I would give them all for such a victory." [64]

Appendix A

"Skirmishing"

For many readers, the thought of eighteenth-century warfare conjures an image of men standing shoulder-to-shoulder, blazing away at relatively short range at an enemy in similar formation. While the image is no doubt accurate for larger conflicts such as Gettysburg, another formal tactic, skirmishing, was at least as common in the Civil War. Although less dramatic in the mind's eye, the relentless skirmishing that engulfed the Bliss Farm reveals that the tactic was an effective – and deadly – form of combat.

Union Skirmish Line Advances at Resaca in 1864 (HW)

Rooted in the tactics of traditional British and French warfare, military training manuals had evolved over time to accommodate the American experience. While the drill differed from manual to manual, in general, "skirmishers" were to advance in company-sized detachments composed of four-man units, with a reserve stationed not far behind. Unlike the conventional massed line of battle, each skirmisher was to advance five paces apart, carefully picking their targets while taking advantage of cover and concealment. In doing so, they could conduct reconnaissance, and as events dictated, prevent their main formations from detection or ambush; in addition, offering a poor target, the open order skirmishing formations could be used as an effective tactic against enemy artillery.

By 1855, W.J. Hardee's, <u>Rifle and Light Infantry Tactics</u>, had become the standard instruction manual for the U.S. Army. Hardee's manual updated earlier versions and, specifically, expanded the use of skirmishers in battle. Earlier manuals called for the training and deployment of one company from each regiment as skirmishers; Hardee expanded the concept, specifying that an entire regiment could form a skirmish line. In effect, Hardee became one of the earliest regular army officers to advocate that large units could advance in less formal, open order formations. On July 2, 1863, Brigadier General Posey employment these regiment-size skirmish lines to effectively drive the 12th New Jersey from the Bliss Farm; however, the less structured advance by the Mississippians would be unable to support Wright's breakthrough.

Appendix B

Wright's "Breakthrough"

When tracing the deployments around the Bliss Farm, and the consequent attack and repulse of Wright's Brigade that evening, it is clear that there were significant problems in the Southern leadership on July 2. And, as the "High Water Mark" of Lee's attack that afternoon, Wright's breakthrough on Cemetery Ridge has generated much discussion and research to determine how successful the Georgians were in penetrating the Union line.

Not surprisingly, one of the most detailed descriptions of what happened that evening comes from Wright himself. As a lawyer and active politician in pre-war Georgia, Ambrose "Rans" Wright had risen through the ranks to brigade command in 1862 and survived wounds at both Chancellorsville and Antietam. Just five days after the action, he wrote to his wife back in Georgia:

> *My brave men pressed rapidly and steadily on, until we approached within fifty or sixty yards of the enemy's batteries, when we encountered a heavy body of infantry posted behind a stone wall. The side of the mountain was so precipitous here that my men could with difficulty climb it, but we strove on, and reaching the stone fence, drove the Yankee infantry from behind it, and then taking cover from the fence we soon shot all the gunners of the enemy's artillery, and rushing over the fence seized the guns. We had now accomplished our task. We had stormed the enemy's strong position, had drove off his infantry, had captured all his guns in our front, except a few which he succeeded in carrying off, and had up to this minute suffered but comparatively small loss.* [1]

In his official report written the following September, Wright then described the scenario in somewhat more detail:

> *My men, by a well-directed fire, soon drove the cannoneers from their guns, and, leaping over the fence, charged up to the top of the crest, and drove the enemy's infantry into a rocky gorge on the eastern slope of the heights, and some 80 or 100 yards in rear of the enemy's batteries.* [2]

Modern view of the rocky ledge in front of the Union position on Cemetery Ridge

Walking up the west slope of Cemetery Ridge, one can well imagine that, with the billowing smoke, the confusion of battle, and the threat of imminent danger, the rocky terrain might appear more precipitous than it actually is; certainly, Wright's unfamiliarity with the ground may well have contributed to his exaggerated memories. That said, Wright's descriptions of his accomplishments still come off as overblown and self-serving, and are easily dismissed as fantasy. Yet, the commander of the Union troops in the area, Brigadier General John Gibbon, agreed with Wright in point:

"The enemy came on with such impetuosity that the head of his column came quite through a vacancy in our line to the left of my division ...." ³

While we may never know the extent of Wright's success, it is clear that Lee's enormous en echelon attack faltered after Wright's advance, and the breakthrough, however successful, lacked coordinated support. The question then becomes: what happened in the Southern leadership on July 2?

Again unfortunately, other than General Wright, there is little detailed evidence, and the reports written by Southern leadership after the battle either are vague or contradictory. Most agree on one point: the Federal counterattacks were overwhelming. This clearly accounts for the failure of Wilcox and Perry's brigades to support Wright's southern flank, and for the Georgians' retreat, but Posey's scattered support is more problematic. Wright later claimed:

> *Just before reaching [the Emmitsburg Road], I had observed that Posey's brigade, on my left, had not advanced, and...I dispatched my aide-de-camp, Capt. R. H. Bell, with a message to Major-General Anderson, informing him of my own advance and its extent, and that General Posey had not advanced with his brigade on my left. To this message I received a reply to press on; that Posey had been ordered in on my left, and that he (General Anderson) would reiterate the order.* ⁴

Posey himself was apparently willing to cooperate, but claimed he was following Anderson's specific orders, and lacked the protection of Mahone's Brigade on his flank:

> *I received an order to advance after Brigadier-General Wright, who was posted on my right in a woods before the*

advance was made. I received an order from the major-general, through his aide-de-camp Captain [S.D.] Shannon, to advance but two of my regiments, and deploy them closely as skirmishers. I had then a thin line of skirmishers in front, and at once sent out the Forty-eighth and Nineteenth Regiments... These regiments advanced some 200 or 300 yards beyond the barn and house, ... Later in the day, I sent out the Sixteenth, and receiving information that the enemy were threatening their right and left flanks, took out the Twelfth Regiment, and requested Brigadier-General Mahone, who was on my left, in the rear of another division, to send me a regiment to support my left. He being at this time ordered to the right, could not comply. When I reached the barn, I found my three regiments well up in advance. They had driven the enemy's pickets into their works and the artillerists from their guns in their front. It being then nearly dark, I sent the major-general a message, informing him of my position. He then ordered me to fall back to my original position, in the rear of Pegram's battery. [5]

Clearly, communication and cooperation broke down at a divisional level. As division commander, Anderson himself should have been able to shed some light on the issue, but merely reported later:

The line of battle was formed, with the brigades in the following order: Wilcox's, Perry's,...Wright's, Posey's, and Mahone's. [I was] ordered to put the troops of my division into action by brigades as soon as those of General Longstreet's corps bad progressed so far in their assault as to be connected with my right flank. ... The advance of McLaws' division was immediately followed by the brigades of mine, in the manner directed. ... They drove the

> *enemy from his first line, and possessed themselves of the ridge and of much of the artillery with which it had been crowned; but the situation discovered the enemy in possession of a second line, with artillery upon both our front and flanks. From this position he poured a destructive fire of grape upon our troops. Strong re-enforcements pressed upon our right flank, which had become disconnected from McLaws' left, and the ridge was untenable. The brigades were compelled to retire. They fell back in the same succession in which they had advanced: Wilcox's, Perry's, Wright's, and Posey's. They regained their positions in the line of battle. The enemy did not follow.* [6]

Clearly, after three hours of combat, stretching from the far side of Little Round Top to the very summit of Cemetery Ridge, and, at perhaps at the most critical moment of July 2, some of Lee's most trusted subordinates came to an impasse. Here again, while is tempting to speculate on why, despite numerous accounts, there appears no clear consensus. While discussing the mystery in his book on July 2, perhaps Gettysburg historian Harry Pfanz said it most succinctly: "Something was wrong in Anderson's division that evening." [7]

Appendix C
ORDER OF BATTLE

The following is a partial Order of Battle listing units described in the text as fighting on the Bliss Farm and vicinity.[1]

Key: (Total Engaged) K-W-M=Total Loss

ARMY OF THE NORTHERN VIRGINIA – Gen. Robert E. Lee

THIRD ARMY CORPS - Lt. Gen. A. P. Hill
ANDERSON'S DIVISION - Maj. Gen. R. H. Anderson
Mahone's Brigade - Brig. Gen. Wm Mahone (1,542)
    6th Virginia (288) 0-4-6=10
    12th Virginia (348) 3-11-8=22
    16th Virginia (270) 2-15-5=22
    41st Virginia (276) 2-10-0=12
    61st Virginia (356) 5-10-0=15

Wright's Brigade - Brig. Gen. A. R. Wright (1,413)
    3rd Georgia (441) 49-139-31=219
    22nd Georgia (400) 41-70-60=171
    48th Georgia (395) 70-97-57=224
    2nd Georgia Battalion (173) 24-37-21=82

Posey's Brigade - Brig. Gen. C. Posey (1,322)
    12th Mississippi (305) 1-11-1=13
    16th Mississippi (385) 3-16-7=26
    19th Mississippi (372) 5-26-3=34
    48th Mississippi (256) 6-27-6=39

PENDER'S DIVISION – Maj. Gen. W.D. Pender
Perrin's Brigade - Col. A. Perrin
    14th South Carolina (428) 27-182 = 209

Scales' Brigade - Brig. Gen. A. M. Scales (1,405)
    13th North Carolina (232) 50-98-26=279
    16th North Carolina (321) 24-61-38=123

22nd North Carolina (321) 37-79-150=166
34th North Carolina (311) 19-55-30=104
38th North Carolina (216) 40-63-27=130

ARTILLERY
11th Ga. Artillery Bn. "The Sumter Artillery"- Maj. J. Lane
   Co. A - Ross (130) 1-11-1=13
   Co. B - Patterson (124) 2-6-1=9
   Co. C - Wingfield (121) 0-18-2=20

ARMY OF THE POTOMAC – Maj. Gen. George G. Meade

SECOND ARMY CORPS - Maj. Gen W.S. Hancock
SECOND DIVISION - Brig. Gen. J. Gibbon
Second Brigade - Brig. Gen. A. S. Webb
   106th Pennsylvania (280) 9-54-1=64

THIRD DIVISION Brig. Gen. A. Hays
First Brigade - Col. S. S. Carroll (942)
   4th Ohio (299) 9-17-5=31
   8th Ohio (209) 18-83-1=102

Second Brigade - Col. T. A. Smyth (1,103)
   14th Connecticut (172) 10-52-4=66
   1st Delaware (251) 10-54-17=77
   12th New Jersey (444) 23-83-9=115
   108th New York (200) 16-86-0=102

Third Brigade - Col. G. L. Willard (1,508)
   39th New York (four co.s) (269) 15-80-0=95
   111th New York (390) 58-177-14=249
   125th New York (392) 26-104-9=139
   126th New York (455) 40-181-10=231

ARTILLERY - Capt. J.G. Hazard
   1st R.I., A, (Arnold) (117) 10-16-0=26
   1st R.I., B, (Brown) (129) 3-28-1=32
   1st U.S., I, (Woodruff) (112) 1-24-0=25
   4th U.S., A, (Cushing) (126) 6-32-0=38

NOTE: Even a cursory review of the above figures suggests that a precise accounting of those engaged at the Bliss property is problematic:

- Skirmishing by its nature was informal; accordingly, not all deployments were reported.
- The totals above generally reflect the entire number engaged/lost, Several regiments saw action on other parts of the field before and after their Bliss Farm action. In addition, some units were deployed in their entirety, others only contributed two companies.
- It is apparent that at least some the figures for the Southern loss are incorrect. By example, it is well documented that at least 90 Southerners were captured by the 12th New Jersey. Although it is likely that most of these were from Posey's 19th and 48th Mississippi, these figures indicate only 17 captured for the entire brigade.
- In lieu of hard numbers, perhaps the cost can be seen best in the 14th Connecticut, a regiment whose actions and numbers are well documented. According to one officer, Farm less Companies B and D (about 30 men on the skirmish line), the regiment had only 100 men after seizing the Bliss Farm; the eight companies in the sortie, then, lost at least 42 men, or about 28%.

In the end, the detailed regimental analysis performed by Woody Christ in <u>The Struggle for the Bliss Farm at Gettysburg</u>, suggests the overall extent of the conflict around the Bliss Farm. [2]

	Engaged	K-W-M	Loss %
Union	2,160	360	17%
Confederate	2,310	470	20%
	4,470	830	

Endnotes

1. Adams County Deed Book, notes in Bliss Farm Vertical File, GNMP; Elwood Christ, "Over a Wide Hot...Crimson Plain" The Struggle for the Bliss Farm, (Baltimore: Butternut & Blue, 1992), pp. 114-7. William Bliss was born in 1799 in Rehoboth, Massachusetts. He married Adeline in 1823, and by 1833, the couple migrated west, finally settling in upstate New York near Jamestown, Chautauqua County. With the marriage of daughter Adeline to Daniel Harris in 1856, it is likely only daughters Sarah and Frances moved to Gettysburg with their parents in 1857.

2. Edwin B. Coddington, The Gettysburg Campaign: A Study in Command, (New York: Charles Scribner's Sons, 1968; Revised and Reprinted, Dayton, Ohio: Morningside, 1979), p. 267; Christ, Struggle, p. 3; George D. Bowen, "Diary of George D. Bowen", Valley Forge Journal, (Vol. 2, #1, July 1984: Copy on file, GNMP Library), p. 130.

3. John B. Bachelder, Map of the Battlefield of Gettysburg, Position of Troops, First & Second Days Battle, (New York: Office of the Chief of Engineers, U.S. Army, 1876); All troop strengths are obtained from John W. Busey & David G. Martin, Regimental Strengths and Losses at Gettysburg, (Hightstown, New Jersey: Longstreet House, 1986).

4. Harry W. Pfanz, Gettysburg: The Second Day (Chapel Hill, N.C.: University of North Carolina Press, 1987), pp. 42, 66; Survivors Association, History of the Corn Exchange Regiment, 118th Pennsylvania Volunteers, (Philadelphia: J.L. Smith, 1905), p. 238.

5. Bachelder, "Official Map of Troop Positions at Gettysburg, July, 1863," (Boston, 1876); Pfanz, 58-61; United States War Department, The War of the Rebellion: A Compilation of Official Records of the Union And Confederate Armies, 70 Vols. in 128 Parts, (Washington, D.C.: Government Printing Office, 1880-1901), Series I, Vol. 27, Part 1, pp. 115, 369, 427, 453 (Hereafter referred to as O.R., Unless noted all information is taken from Series I, Vol. 27);

6. Charles D. Page, History of the Fourteenth Regiment, Connecticut Volunteer Infantry, (Meriden: Horton Print Company, 1906), p. 138.

7. Ezra D. Simons, A Regimental History: The 125th New York State Volunteers (New York: Simons, 1888) 102-3.

8. O.R., Part 1, pp. 453, 477; Samuel W. Fiske, Mr. Dunn Browne's Experiences in the Army, (Boston: Nichols & Noyes, 1866), p. 182. Captain of Co. G, at Gettysburg, 34 yr-old Fiske was previously minister of a Congregational church in Madison, CT. Formerly from Central Massachusetts, Fiske wrote a series of letters to the *Springfield Republican* newspaper under the pen name "Dunn Brown".

9. New York Monuments Commission for the Battlefields of Gettysburg and Chattanooga, Final Report of the Battlefield of Gettysburg, 3 Volumes, (Albany: J.B. Lyon Company Printers, 1900), p. 2: 800, 882 (hereafter referred to as N.Y. at Gettysburg).

10. Page, History, p. 138-9; O.R., Part 2, p. 671; Henry S. Stevens, Address Delivered at the Dedication of the Monument of the 14th Connecticut Volunteers at Gettysburg, Penn., July 3d, 1884, (Middletown, CT: Pelton & King, 1884), p.15. At Gettysburg, Scales' brigade was composed of the 13th, 16th, 22nd, 34th, and 38th NC regiments.

11. O.R., Part 1, p. 460; Joseph R. Ward, History of the One Hundred and Sixth Regiment, Pennsylvania Volunteers, (Philadelphia: F. McManus Jr. & Co., 1906), p. 186; Fiske, Dunn Browne, p.182.

12. George T. Fleming, The Life and Letters of General Alexander Hays, (Pittsburgh: No Publ.,1919), pp. 267, 335; Pfanz, The Second Day, p. 65.

13. Pfanz, The Second Day, p. 67; John Bachelder Papers, Letter from Captain C.A. Richardson to John Bachelder, August 8, 1886, New Hampshire Historical Society, Concord, N.H., Copy on file at GNMP Library.

14. Stevens, Address, p. 16; Fleming, Hays, p. 431; O.R., Part 1, p.472.

15. Page, <u>History</u>, pp. 142-144.
16. Ibid; Richardson Letter.
17. <u>O.R.</u>, Part 2, pp. 358-9, 614; Edwin B. Coddington, <u>The Gettysburg Campaign: A Study in Command</u>, (New York: Charles Scribner's Sons, 1968; Revised and Reprinted, Dayton, Ohio: Morningside, 1979), pp. 378-80.
18. <u>O.R.</u>, Part 2, p. 614,671; Douglas S. Freeman, <u>Lee's Lieutenants</u>, 3 Volumes, (New York: Charles Scribner's Sons, 1949-51), p. xxxviii, 374, 665. Anderson's left was held by Mahone's Brigade, followed by Posey, Wright, Lang and Wilcox's brigades.
19. <u>O.R.</u>, Part 2, p. 633; Pfanz, <u>The Second Day</u>, p. 67; Diary of James J. Kirkpatrick, July 2, 1863, Transcribed Copy in 16th Mississippi Vertical File, GNMP Library. Posey's Brigade consisted of the 12th, 16th, 19th, 48th Mississippi.
20. Henry S. Stevens, Souvenir of Excursion to Battlefields by the Society of the Fourteenth Connecticut Regiment and Reunion at Antietam, (Washington, D.C.: Gibson Bros., 1893), p. 16.
21. Prof. Michael Jacobs, "Gettysburg Weather Reports," <u>Blue & Gray</u>, (November, 1987), p. 23; Survivors Association of the 118th PA. Volunteers, <u>History of the 118th Pennsylvania Volunteers</u>, (Philadelphia: J.L. Smith, 1905), p. 238; <u>O.R.</u>, Part 1, pp.368, 482-3, 531-2; <u>O.R.</u>, Part 2, pp. 308, 318-9.
22. Page, <u>History</u>, p.144; Stevens, <u>Souvenir</u>, 16. By this account, the current Codori Barn is larger, but similar in appearance. Expanded since 1863, that barn is now approximately 82' L x 43' W and stands 18' to the eaves.
23. Simons, <u>History</u>, p. 102; Jacobs, <u>Reports</u>; <u>Blue & Gray</u>, p. 23; Pfanz, <u>The Second Day</u>, p. 67; John Bachelder Papers, Letter from Captain George Price to John W. Dunn, Copy on file GNMP; Bowen, <u>Diary</u>, pp. 128-9. The battle strength of the 1st Delaware is listed as 251 men. The figure for the 12th New Jersey is 444, which indicates a company strength of roughly 40 men. According to these figures, the detachment at the Bliss property likely numbered about 290 members.

24. James Duffy et al., <u>Final Report of the Gettysburg Battlefield Commission of New Jersey</u>, (Trenton: John Murphy Publ., 1891), pp.110-1.

25. <u>O.R.</u>, Part 2, p. 633; Price Letter; Bowen, <u>Diary</u>, p. 129. According to Busey & Martin, the battle strength of the 16th, 19th, and 48th Mississippi totaled 1019 men.

26. <u>O.R.</u>, Part 1, p. 469; Bowen, <u>Diary</u>, p. 129.

27. Ward, <u>History</u>, p. 191. According to accounts of the 12th New Jersey and 106th Pennsylvania, a large part of the 16th Mississippi occupied the buildings at this point.

28. <u>O.R.</u>, Part 1, p. 464-5,470; Duffy, <u>Final Report</u>, p. 109,112; Letter from Corporal Christopher Mead, Copy in 12th New Jersey Vertical File, GNMP library. Various accounts number the sortie from 100 to 200 members. With a battle strength of 444 men, four companies of the 12th likely numbered close to 150 men.

29. Duffy, <u>Final Report</u>, pp. 109-12; Albert Stokes Emmell Letter for 7/17/63, 12th New Jersey Vertical File GNMP Library. Unlike most units at Gettysburg, the 12th New Jersey was armed with .69 caliber Model 1842 smoothbore muskets. In addition to standard musket balls, the weapon could fire "buck and ball" – a package containing a ball and three buckshot. Although limited in range, the hitting power of such a weapon is obvious.

30. <u>O.R.</u>, Part 1, p. 470.

31. Coddington, <u>Gettysburg</u>, pp. 383, 399-406; <u>O.R.</u>, Part 2, p. 614, 622. The reported time of the advance varies from 5:00 p.m. to 6:30 p.m.; the latter makes more sense in terms of related actions on the field.

32. <u>O.R.</u>, Part 1, p. 470; <u>O.R.</u>, Part 2, pp. 623, 630,663; John Y. Foster, <u>New Jersey in the Rebellion,</u> (Newark: M.R. Dennis & Co., 1868), p. 304; Duffy, <u>Final Report</u>, p. 112.

33. Coddington, <u>Gettysburg</u>, pp. 401-2; <u>O.R.</u>, Part 1, p. 417,423; Pfanz, <u>The Second Day,</u>, pp. 375-6; Andrew E. Ford, <u>The Story of the Fifteenth Regiment, Massachusetts Volunteer Infantry</u>, (Clinton, MA: Press of W.J. Coulter, 1898), p. 267.

34. Freeman, <u>Lee's Lieutenants</u>, 3:125-6; <u>O.R.</u>, Part 2, pp. 622-3.

35. O.R., Part 2, pp. 613, 633-4.

36. O.R., Part 1, pp. 417, 427; N.Y. at Gettysburg, 2:663; Harold R. Barker, History of Rhode Island Units in the Civil War, (No Publ., 1964), p. 185.

37. O.R., Part 1, p. 417; O.R., Part 2, pp. 623, 634; Ford, 15th Massachusetts, pp.267-9; Barker, Rhode Island Units, p. 185.

38. O.R., Part 1, pp. 417, 427; Pfanz, The Second Day, p. 387; Paul A. Hutton, Editor, Gettysburg: Oates and Haskell, (New York: Bantam Books, 1992; Reprint of Frank A. Haskell's "Battle of Gettysburg"), pp. 175-6

39. O.R., Part 1, pp. 417, 447; Jno. Robertson, Michigan in the War, (Lansing, Michigan: W.S. George, Stage Printers, 1880), p. 105; Pfanz, The Second Day, p.420

40. O.R., Part 2, pp. 618, 621, 631-4; Freeman, Lee's Lieutenants, 3:126-8.

41. O.R., Part 1, p. 427; O.R., Part 2, pp. 623-4; Ward, History of the 106th PA., pp. 191-2.

42. Ward, History of the 106th PA., pp. 195-6; Coddington, Gettysburg, p. 427.

43. O.R., Part 2, p. 624; Freeman, Lee's Lieutenants, 3:176; Ward, History of the 106th PA., p.192; John Bachelder Papers, Letter of William E. Potter, Dated 6/10/86, New Hampshire Historical Society, Concord, N.H., Copy on File GNMP Library.

44. O.R., Part 2, p. 634; Terrence J. Winschel, "Posey's Brigade at Gettysburg, Part 2," Gettysburg Magazine, #5 (July, 1991), p. 99.

45. N.Y. at Gettysburg, 2: 664; Page, History, p. 142-3. Huxham, 26 years old, left his wife of less than two years, Carrie, and a 12 month-old son back in Middletown.

46. Duffy, Final Report, pp. 110, 113, 116. The times described for the advance vary from 7:30 a.m. to 10:00 a.m. In light of other actions, 9:00 a.m. seems likely.

47. Duffy, Final Report, pp. 111-2. Cpl. Abel Shute was a 22 year-old farmer from Mullica Hill; carried back to Cemetery Ridge, he died of his wounds on July 31st at a hospital in Baltimore, MD.

48. O.R., Part 2, pp. 659, 663, 666; Duffy, Final Report, p.113.

49. Ibid.
50. Duffy, <u>Final Report</u>, pp. 116-7, Foster, <u>New Jersey</u>, p. 304.
51. Diary of James J. Kirkpatrick, July 3, 1863, Transcribed Copy in 16th Mississippi Vertical File, GNMP Library; Stevens, <u>Address</u>, p. 18; Stevens, <u>Souvenir</u>, p. 18.
52. Page, <u>History</u>, p. 144; Stevens, <u>Souvenir</u>, pp.17-8.
53. Stevens, <u>Souvenir</u>, pp. 18-20.
54. Ibid., p. 19; Alexander McNeil Letter, <u>CWTI</u> Collection, Copy in 14th Connecticut Vertical File, GNMP Library.
55. Ibid.
56. Stevens, <u>Souvenir</u>, pp. 20-1.
57. John Bachelder Papers, Letter from Alexander Hays to Governor Horatio Seymour, Dated 8/15/63, New Hampshire Historical Society, Concord, N.H., Copy on file, GNMP Library.
58. Stevens <u>Souvenir</u>, p. 21; Stevens, <u>Address</u>, p. 19; W.F. Beyer & O.F. Keydel, <u>Deeds of Valor</u>, (Detroit: Perrien - Keydel Co., 1907, Transcript on File, GNMP Library), Vol. 1, pp. 228-9. Captain Postles would receive a Medal of Honor for his actions dated July 2, 1863; however, as described by several members of the 14th Connecticut, his ride took place on July 3. As Postles would doubtless remember two such rides, the actual date of the ride is in question. Years later, however, Postles described passing a group of Southern prisoners behind the ridge, when one spoke up: "Well sir, I guess your time hain't come yet." Asked what he meant, the Rebel replied, "Well I had three fair shots at you, and there are plenty more fellows here who had as many." Capt. Postles had ridden so close to the Southerners, he was easily recognized by them.
59. Stevens, <u>Souvenir</u>, pp. 19, 21-2; Connecticut Adjutant General's Office, <u>Catalogue of Connecticut Volunteer Organizations in the Service of the United States, 1861-5</u>, (Hartford: Brown & Gross, 1869), pp. 555, 570, 574, 576, 579.
60. Stevens, <u>Souvenir</u>, pp. 18, 22; Stevens <u>Address</u>, p.18.
61. Stevens, <u>Souvenir</u>, p. 22.
62. Christ, Struggle, p. 118-21.

63. Ibid.
64. Timothy H. Smith, "'These Were Days of Horror' The Story of the Gettysburg Civilians," *Fifth Annual Gettysburg Seminar, Gettysburg National Military Park* (National Park Service, 1996) n. 32.

Appendix A
William J. Hardee, Hardee's Rifle and Light Infantry Tactics. Volume II. (Government Printing Office, 1855); Kent J. Goff, "The Evolution of Skirmish Tactics in the U.S. Civil War," *Mississippi Valley Educational Programs*,
(http://www.mvep.org/skirmishold.htm);

Appendix B
1. Douglas Southall Freeman, Lee's Lieutenants: A Study in Command, Vol.3, (New York; Charles Scribner's Sons, 1944) p. 126.
2. O.R., Part 2, p. 623.
3. O.R., Part 1, p. 417.
4. O.R., Part 2, p. 623.
5. O.R., Part 2, p. 634.
6. O.R., Part 2, p. 614.
7. Pfanz, The Second Day, p. 386

Appendix C
1. Composition and casualties are from: John W. Busey & David G. Martin, Regimental Strengths and Losses at Gettysburg, (Hightstown, New Jersey: Longstreet House, 1986).
2. Christ, Struggle, p. 97-108.

Index

Anderson, Maj. Gen. Richard H., 27 *bio*, 29*p*, 40, 43, 47, 66, 67, 68, 69, 74

Bliss Farm (described), 13, 28, 34, 35, 54
Bliss, William, 11, 12, 13, 16, 26, 34, 60, 72
Bowen, Sgt. Henry, 36, 37, 72, 74, 75
Brian Farm, 19, 21 *p* (described), 59
Brian, Abraham, 21

Cemetery Hill, 16, 18, 48, 49
Cemetery Ridge, 17, 19, 21, 24, 33, 34, 42, 43, 47, 48, 53, 55, 57, 59, 64, 65, 68, 76
Codori Farm, 42, 44, 45, 46, 60, 74
Confederate Regiments
  2nd Georgia Batt., 41, 69
  3rd Georgia, 69
  22nd Georgia, 69
  48th Georgia, 42, 69
  12th Mississippi, 49, 69
  16th Mississippi, 36, 49, 69, 74, 75, 77
  19th Mississippi, 20, 43, 45, 69
  48th Mississippi, 30, 36, 43, 69, 71, 74, 75

  13th North Carolina, 69
  16th North Carolina, 69
  22nd North Carolina, 70
  34th North Carolina, 70
  38th North Carolina, 70
  14th South Carolina, 69

Ellis, Maj. Theodore, 55, 56
Emmitsburg Road, 19, 21, 24, 26, 29, 30, 31, 40, 42, 43, 44, 45, 49, 50, 54, 55, 58, 66

Federal Regiments
  Carroll's Brigade, 19, 48, 49, 70
  1st Delaware, 22, 25, 36, 37, 57, 70, 74
  14th Connecticut, 18, 22, 25, 26, 34, 38, 48, 49, 52, 53, 55, 70, 71, 73, 77
  12th New Jersey, 25, 36, 38, 40, 48, 50, 63, 70, 71, 74, 75
  39th New York, 24, 25, 70
  111th New York, 25, 57, 70
  125th New York, 22, 35, 70, 73
  126th New York, 26, 70
  8th Ohio, 31, 70
  1st R.I., Batt. B, (Brown) 44, 45, 46, 47, 70, 73, 76, 77

1st U.S., Batt. I, (Woodruff). 18, 19, 70

Gibbon, Brig. Gen. John, 19, 42, 44, 45, 46, 47, 48, 65, 70

Hancock, Maj. Gen Winfield, 17, 19, 21, 25, 30, 37, 42, 48, 70
Harris Family (Bliss Descendants), 8, 72
Harris, Lt. Col. Edward, 36
Hays, Brig. Gen. Alexander, 18, 22, 23*p*, 24 *bio*, 26, 36, 39, 42, 48, 53, 54, 57, 70, 73, 77
Hill, Lt. Gen. A. P., 16, 27, 40, 49, 54, 69, 72, 76

Jobes, Capt. Samuel, 40

Lee, Gen. Robert E., 16, 17, 27, 43, 48, 59, 64, 66, 68, 69, 74, 75, 76, 78

Longstreet, Lt. Gen. James, 27, 31, 35, 40, 67, 72, 78
Lynch, Capt. James, 38

Meade, Maj. Gen. George G., 17, 18, 27, 70
Moore, Capt. Samuel, 54

Pender's Division, 41, 51, 55, 69
Perrin, Col. Abner, 51, 69
Posey, Brig, Gen. Carnot, 29*p*, 30 *bio*, 36, 37, 40, 41, 43, 45, 47, 48, 49, 63, 66, 67, 69, 71, 74, 76
Postles, Capt. James, 57, 77

Skirmishers, 22, 23, 26, 30, 33, 36, 37, 41, 43, 51, 62-63, 67

Wright, Brig. Gen. Ambrose, 40, 41 *p*, 42, 43, 44, 45, 46, 47, 48, 49, 59, 63, 64 *bio*, 65, 66, 67, 69, 74

Made in the USA
Lexington, KY
15 March 2013